How To Succeed At Being Funny Without Trying By

Professor PMS

<u>Hint</u>: in order to become a lousier, i.e., better Comedian you have to <u>practice</u>, <u>practice</u>, <u>and practice</u> your comedy all the time and listen to the tapes you make in a recorder or that you write down on a 3X5 Card. You can choose from Physical Comedy, Stand Up Comedy w/ a 3X5 Card or Improvisation (making stuff up on the spot) or any other kind of comedy that is preferably <u>memorized</u>. Committing your comedy to <u>memory</u> means that you really did something good as you can't screw it up unless of course you get drunk, high or distracted before the show happens. BAD IDEA: Stay Sober and have a drink of whatever beverage you like drinking AFTER THE SHOW HAPPENS: that's your REWARD FOR DOING A LOUSY or GREAT JOB. Make sure that before you decide to show up to a Comedy Club that you know the following: Comedy Clubs & Comedians who run show <u>DISCRIMINATE</u> AGAINST EVERYBODY & find out what the <u>RULES</u> are before you decide to just show up out of the blue: it pays to be prepared in advance of showing up expecting to get put on the stage. That just won't cut it. You have to practice your "unfunny" comedy any chance you get and just because a joke worked in one club doesn't mean that it's going to work in another club as the night always changes and so do the clientele that go to Comedy Clubs all over the world. Being a "Comedian" is like a 'One Nite Stand' every time you go: <u>your funny/fun loving lover is your audience</u>. It's up to you to write or find jokes that you've rehearsed in front of people so you can know what does and doesn't work. Practicing your craft is like learning how to create a "Craft Beer", to make a cabinet or learning how to sing on key thru a broken nose. <u>REMEMBER</u>: your "Comedy Career" is not going to become a career in the finest sense of the words written here unless it's meant to be. You want to get paid for your comedy: write a book, make an Audio Book or bring a hat or sand pail with you when you perform your act and hand it out to any Audience Member, not the person ruining the show, I mean running the show. Chances are that the person who is running the "Comedy Show" that night is <u>being paid</u> by the owner of the bar/club/venue or at the very least the person who is running the bar for the evening. It's best to focus

on becoming an "Amateur Comedian" and not a "Professional Stand Up Comedian" as that implies your being <u>PAID</u> regularly and you know that isn't happening anytime soon unless you follow what I just wrote a few sentences back about getting paid for your hard earned writing and Potty Mouth, i.e., diarrhea of the potty mouth; coming up with a set list that you know works for you and not necessarily your audience is what you need to do. Not everybody is meant succeed all the time: that's the beauty of being a "Stand-Up Comedian": you get to keep doing it when there are shows available and practicing your craft is what's going to get you <u>INVITED TO OTHER COMEDY CLUBS OUTSIDE OF WHEREVER YOU LIVE</u>. When you fail miserably with your material just remember that you can always break out the worst joke in the world: it's called '<u>The Aristocrats Joke</u>': throw that at your audience in a really high pitched voice: make it sound like you had sex w/ your whole family in any way, shape or form to bring your audience back to listening to you and you will become a successful comedian. Make sure that you moan and groan as the Audience is <u>GUARANTEED TO LAUGH NO MATTER WHAT</u>. Remember that after you have brought out this "little shop of horrors story/joke" that your audience is going to really want to "kill" your comedy set so make sure that you get back to your "Set List" and give it all you've got. That's the Rule #1. <u>SECRET</u> to becoming a good comedian: keep failing until you get what you want out of speaking to an audience and making them laugh when you do your "Comedy Sets". Eventually, you will get really good at being a sucksexful (successful) comedian: It's not that your material sucks: did you ever think that you suck at being funny and that's why you want to become a successful comedian??? You have a major case of low-self esteem & the best thing you can do here is: <u>Forget About having Low-Self Esteem</u>: sublimate your darn <u>EGO</u> and live your life anyways: that's why you are <u>HERE NOW</u> reading this book. You don't like this book or your life??? It could be 50++ Times WORSE: Become a Grateful Person: The <u>ONLY</u> Person responsible for making you funny is <u>YOU</u>: sweet, wonderful you. You can always give this unfunny comedy book to somebody as a gift to somebody that you like or don't like: then the book will end up in somebody else's hands and they'll read it and laugh their a** off…Keep Sucking Because You Can Only Suck For So Long and then you will become a "good successful" Stand-Up Comedian at some point in the game: making people laugh is no easy feat: you just have to keep trying until you succeed at being the funny person you know yourself to be: you are going to have good nights and bad nights as a "Stand-Up Comedian" and sometimes what you think is funny won't be funny at all and you're going to completely bomb in front of your audience. That's 'The Death of A Comedian': All "Comedy Clubs" or "Amateur Nights"

<u>**DISCRIMINATE AGAINST COMEDIANS**</u>: this is the kind of world we live in all things being UNEQUAL. 'every successful comedian in the world has their good nights and their bad nights'. That's the life of a Stand-Up Comedian. Don't let that bother you. Rule #2 about becoming a good comedian: if all else has failed and you know that you suck at being a Comedian you can always yell everything at your Audience as then you are <u>GUARANTEED TO MAKE YOUR AUDIENCE LAUGH</u>: it won't matter what you are saying because the audience is going to think that you are pissed off at the world and that isn't such a bad place to be in now is it? It works for <u>**Lewis Black**</u>: he always sounds like he's having a '**Bad Life**' and like he's going to have a heart attack or something worse. You can also buy a book thru Amazon or any other site about how to become a Successful Comedian in the World of Comedian as there are millions of starving comedians out there: the goal is to compete w/ yourself and not the comedians you are "up against". Remember that you are just trying to make people laugh in a world full of haters, masturbators and what not. You can also hang out with a group of Comedians by taking "A Course in Comedy Miracles" for 300 and you'll get 9 classes and get a "Certificate in Comedy". Not such a bad idea when you want to pay to learn the secrets of becoming a funny successful comedian in a cut-throat world of mercenaries who don't give a rats ass if you succeed or fail trying to be funny: it's all on you and I Believe In Your Ability To Become FUNNY: break a leg if you must. Eventually, persistence will pay off and you will break through to being a funny comedian. It's only a matter of time when that happens. Rule #3: Make sure that you laugh 50++ Times Per Day to keep up the dopamine levels you need in your body so that you can keep being a Funny Man or a Funny Woman…Rule #4: Buy this book, come up with a comedy set based on what I wrote for the jokes that appeal to you like a slippery banana and use these jokes in your Comedy Act. How am I going to know that you stole my BEST MATERIAL??? I won't and I give you complete permission to do this. Also, buying this book to use in your "Stand-Up/Improvisation Comedy Act" is a start.

I'm a grouper fish: I eat everything in site: I'm the garbage disposal of the seas. Does anybody know why fish eat fish??? Human beings are like this but in a different way. It's called a 'Hostile Takeover'

If you know what I mean: huh, what??? What do you mean??? Are you trying to be funny again and failing at that???!!! You have to keep trying until you actually succeed at sucking seed…something like that…

I Deserve to Be Loved: but frequently all I get is bullshit.

You have the nicest smile I've seen in quite some time: and you're teeth are just so white: do you use cum to floss them and keep them white??? I sure do...I floss my teeth with your dick every day to keep them cleaner and whiter...

When Will I Be Love: and if you are not loved then what will you do??? Like Intel says, "It's All Inside".

You Are Loved: are you faking serious: get outta hear...

I come from **ROYALTY**: I have blue blood...not red until it hits the air...

It will take more than a cursory apology for Josh Hader to put this behind him

I'm sure that he'll enjoy being bent over the coffee table and being forced to take B*g Bl*ck D*ck up his A** and being B*tched Sl*pp*d by a bunch of angry Amazonian women who are out for blood and then also being forced to suck some really hard cock by his teammates before this is all over...besides, he's really cute and you know how it goes with cute guys: they're the ones who usually have the most to hide who are busy smashing the picture any chance they get...and, fucking your father, brother or uncle behind the Maine Mall near one of those green cummy nasty dirty filthy cum dumpsters.

Where do overweight people work: at a donut factory, a whale factory processing whale meat, an all you can eat buffet...they also watch 'The Fat Albert Cartoon' regularly as it makes them feel better...

Where do thin people work: at a Soup Kitchen, at The Slim Shady Rap Factory, a Diet Factory, a Juice Factory...they also listen to that record from the 60's: The Story of Fatboy Slim on a 45 rpm...

9 Words that start with a 'C' that are funny:
9. **Cordial**
8. **Compact**
7. **Closemouthed**
6. **Civilized**
5. **Chirpy**

4. **Callous**
3. **Contentious**
2. **Cantankerous**
1. **Curmudgeon**
And, you thought I was going to say "cunts" or "those cocksuckers". Well, I did. Anybody know of any funny words that start with the word 'C'???

If there was a phone up me arse I'd hear it vibrate when it rang 69 times...

If there was a cell phone up your ass you'd feel it vibrate when it rang and then your asshole could answer it for you!!!

I'm a minority as I'm "straight" & "straight to bed". I'll fuck anywhere I darn well please, especially in a church, a mortuary, any place that is PUBLIC w/o getting caught...I'm 'The Material Boy' & my name's not **MDNA** butt I'm a lot of fun to be with and I love sucking a hot hard cock from a guy who's **So Serious** about getting his nut off in me or on me...**TRY ME**: who wants to make **Nut Butter** in my butt???

Susan Harris I accidentally erased some requests for friends. I am sorry. Please post me again. **Ashley Lenartson** I'll definitely being posting you all over the Internet...ha ha ha ha ha ha ha...

Cliff Springer sent me a pick of his hard cut dick thru facebook so I replied: "I'd definitely suck that off and eat your manhole out by spreading it wide for my lips and more...you make me so horny, so horny..."

<u>Man you have a beautiful cock says Cliff Springer</u>
it's around 8" when pumped up; I pump it up as often as I can...I'm working on stretching out my mankunt with the widest frozen cu cum ber I've been able to get up there was 7" around...I didn't think it would go up there on account of the bump in it but it was mighty fine when I finally was able to push it through my back door...it definitely made me go, "OHHHH..." It felt good to do...I was so hot and turned on I just blew my load right then and there...

I'm working on my piles every day and condensing a lot of stuff into less and less and in boxes that expand ever more...I just put a bunch of dress shirts back on hangers and made more room in my closet so I can go back in there and sleep at night…ha ha ha ha ha...I guess I'm now officially a **'Closet Case'**...this just proves that I'm a homosexual sapien.

Welcome to Portland, Maine: The Ass End of The Universe

I once went to an AA Meeting with a 30 Pack of Beer from Schlitz. They asked me to leave as I was causing a commotion. So, I left the 30 pack of beer behind as I don't drink alcohol.

I'm THE Star of my own show...that's how it is with me: and, I can share the stage with as many people as possible...

When I get an erection I pass out from all the blood going to my **Oscar Meyer Weiner**

I did some heavy lifting last night: I lifted my boyfriend's balls into my mouth

John Hagee: "God made all lesbians flat so they could be identified by normal people easily."
He only says those disparaging things as he's really a lesbian and he can't come to terms with his feelings...He also loves it when his wife of 30++ years puts the strap-on on and plunges it deep into his mangina...she leaves it a gaping messed up hole by the time she gets through with it... He should know as he's very flat chested and identifies with God judging people because of his religious beliefs and he's really s **'Closet Case for the Gay Community'**. He's definitely a rug burner and a **'Secret Homosexual'**...

Why was Sunday Mass cancelled? Nun showed up

I don't do drugs: they do me

I'm an endless buffet: who wants to devour me???

HELP HELP HELP: I'm in the **Military** and I need **MONEY**. Can you send me an I-Tunes Card right now???

12-Pound Rat found in a gutter on a street in London! That looks like one of my long lost relatives…

© Tony Smith/SWNS.com

**Sometimes you can be
Your own worst enemy or
Your own best friend.
I have amnesia so I don't know who I AM...**

Don't you just love it when you get a message from Nigeria or wherever and somebody tells you that you just won a million dollars and all you have to do is send a fee??? It goes on and on and one with this bullshit online: will it ever stop??? I ask for their address and I send them a mail bomb: problem finished. The FBI came knocking at my door the other day so I left a special package behind the door for them and made sure it was turned on very loudly. I can't understand why they had to call in '**The Bomb Squad**'. Was that really necessary???!!! I was doing the world a favor by getting rid of **Professional Con-Artists**.

Crack some jokes that you think are funny or bend over and laugh at yourself in the mirror...

Hey Babe: What am I??? A PIG???

When I was growing up my mother used to be called '**The Milky Way**'

When I was growing up my step-father was known for being '**Long Dong Whitey**'

My mother once bought a blow up doll for me: I promptly blew it up with my penis. Then I gave it back to her for a <u>**REFUND**</u>.

I was born in a box but I won't go out in a box

or, is it **SPANK YOU VERY MUCH**??? I do not know...Have a Happy Day Laughing your butt off...that's what I do to keep me from going insane in the membrain... **JOKES sh*t**...that's just the way it is with him. He's my famous artist relative, all things being relative...

TO MAKE YOU P*SS YOUR PANTS/PANTIES:

<u>**Jokes for Prostitutes**</u>

What did the prosty say to the client as she was leaving? Come Again!

Why do prostys stick together? They believe in hot liquids.

What wood you do when invited to a convention of prostys? Hope to get laid…

How many prostitutes does it take to change a light bulb??? One to screw it in and the other 4 to say, "Is it in yet???" or "That's not tight or big enough. Then somebody says, "Let me try screwing the light bulb in **N E X T**." "Only the biggest will do…"

Praise be, praise though, I'm a phat cow…who wants to fuck a phat cow? 'Yo ma'ma: looks like you like phat cows.

My name's **Dic Tater**. I rule my own **EMPIRE**!!!

I'm po, so I'ma ho. That's all there is to it. I'm a ho who wants some 'mo. an I want another 'ho bag! Are there any ho's in the audience. Announce yourself and step right up. I think we can make a deal…

I have a new boyfriend: his name's Ben A Dryl. Please acknowledge his presence next time you see him. He's very hawt. You'd like him! I once took a a Ben A Dryl pill and I fell asleep in a friends bed and when I woke up I felt like I was drunk and I didn't know if I was going to be able to make it home: I felt ***that*** drunk.

My artist name is **Billy Lipschitz**. I'm very famous in my own head. I have relatives here in America and across the pond…I'm related to that other famous artist by the name of **Lipschitz**…all that comes out of his mouth is funny words or shit when he's in a pissed off mood.

There are so many Emotional/Spiritual Changes going on on in this planet that you simply cannot believe everything that that media throws at you. It's best to surround yourself w/ people who care about & love you. Everybody else can take a hike on a very long path off a short pier...I do mean **THAT**...it's just that at my age I don't have any time for **B.S.** as I don't like **B.S.** being thrown in my face. That's why I act out a good portion of the time...You can check out my very funny comedy book thru **https://tinyurl.com/d4msmg8**...when you purchase the book I'm going to send you a **<u>BONUS</u>** thru the mail. Just show me the receipt and I'll do that a.s.a.p. **JUST 4 U**!!! Go Now, Laugh Your Butt Off Today...While I was busy growing up all over the world my step-fathers tour of duty in Germany came to an end and my whole family was flown back to the Newark New Jersey Airport. I had to settle for the fact that things were going to be different now, much different. One day when I was in grammar school in the 7th Grade: Our 7th Grade Teacher, Maurice Pelletier, asked the class what a **Black Hole** was and the whole class pointed at me during Science Class. Then he turned to me and asked me where the **Grand Canyon** was located and I pointed to **Paula M** and the whole class erupted in laughter. It was then that I knew I'd become a **Professional Stand Up Comedian** and tell jokes for a living...a good friend of mine, **Sarah R**, asked me to take her on a whale watch and I told her to give me $30.00. She asked me what would be the best time to go on a whale watch so I said, "Let's go right now during the middle of the day." I packed her in my truck and off we went. When I got to Congress Street I said, "Do you see any whales walking down the street???" She said, "That's not a whale watch." I said, "Yes, it is." She protested. I told her to get out of my boat as I was driving down Congress Street and made her walk home. As far as I'm concerned we were on a Whale Watch. Why pay $30.00 to go out on a boat that mite conk out on your 'El Capitain' for no particular reason or God forbid, one of the whales decides it doesn't like humans and decides to capsize the boat full of whales trying to get a good picture of them??? Shouldn't it be the other way 'round??? My aim as a 'Professional Comedian' is to be Politically Incorrect. That's what comedians do. I love making people laugh...This is a great book to have close by in any room of the house as it will be **<u>Guaranteed Laughs</u>** and you will end up w/ a smile on your face when you feel you are at the lowest point in your life and that you simply can't go on...**Go Now: Read the book and laugh your butt off then make that purchase**. The book won't break the bank and you will thank me later. Sincerely, Professor Snotty Potty Mouth Syndrome UnLtd **<u>ONLY</u>** 5.95 for a Limited Time until the end of this month. Laughter IS The Best Medicine...

Where else can one go online and send naked pix of themselves to people all around the world besides a sex site that is geared for that??? The beauty of the Internet…what a glorious way to waste a day when you aren't working at your job(s) making money.

let me know when you want your big racket sucked off to cumpletion. I know you winked@ME! Does this mean you like my big phat daddy dink??? **I'm a Cumedian**...I like to cum a lot from making people laugh their butts off... https://tinyurl.com/cdvvejp '**Confessions of A Dirty Man Whore**' _**ONLY**_ 9.95 EA **FREE PREVIEW** for guys like **YOU**...Daddy came over last night and banged me so hard I thought I was going to take flight, then when he was about to cum he said, "Where do you want it?" I said, "Pull it out and shove your 'Daddy Dong' in my mouth and I'll suck all your baby batter out..." He said, "Oh boy, you're going to make me cum, you're my hot manboy, oh here it cums, Daddy's going to give it to you straight from the tap are you ready you '**Wild & Crazy Guy**' Boy???" I said, "Oh Daddy, just do it, I can't wait for you to cum in my hot Party Mouth just get that hot man butter out of your cocksnout..." ... You enjoy **PRIDE** this year...hope to see you at Deering Oaks this Saturday from 7am-6pm...I'll be selling my wares. You are welcome to ask me for a **FREE** Bead Necklace or a sticker for your car, etc. **PEACE & HOT LOVE!!! R.S.V.P.** 207-239-7048 .**TXT ME PLEASE...CIAO BABY! CIAO!**
JOKES TO MAKE YOU COMFORTABLE IN YOUR OWN SKIN: I yam a very funny guy. This is how I know to be a true said thing.

I told somebody that I was very funny and they said, "Tell me a very funny joke." I said, "I forgot all my jokes." They said, "Come on, tell me a very funny joke. I don't care if it sucks, just tell me a very good joke I can sink my teeth into..." I said, "the other night I heard a really big bang. I thought it was my sister." They laughed. They then said, "Do you have any more funny jokes." I said, "Of corpse I do. What do you think you are doing? Talking to a dead man?" They said, "Are you a ghost?" I said, "I might be." Then I said, "Ok, so you want to hear funny jokes, huh?" They said, "You did tell me that you're a very funny person." So I said, "I was visiting a friend the other day and they wouldn't stop talking so I turned off the tv." They said, "Why did you do that?" I said, "As long as you are going to keep talking so that I cannot hear the program on the boob tube I may as well turn it off." He said, "Why is that?" I said, "Well, since I'm just here to listen to the program and you keep talking we may as well keep talking." He said, "Ok, since you insist..." I then said, "After we are done talking for a whole hour, I'm going to make out a bill in the amount of 120.00 so that I can submit it to you on account of the fact that you won't stop talking to me like I'm your therapist." He laughed. I turned the television back on when I left.

Now that I've made you laugh your butt off why don't you go and check out the following link: **happyendingsinmaine.blogspot.com** thru blogspot.com A Happy Ending can be anything you like. It really can be and not just the obvious...Tell US what you don't like about the website and we'll be glad to get right back to you right away. You are welcome to e-mail: **bbbillybigbe94@gmail.com** or **Maverick Ashley Lenartson** 198 Sherwood St 3 Portland ME 04103 207 239 7048 Thank You very much for your time and cooperation in this business matter...I specialize in the following: writing songs, healing (REIKI/Metaphysical/Massage Techniques), Making Art, Writing/Research –I can edit out your Manuscript, Writing, College Papers for 4.00 a page –writing comedy, Adult Stories for Mature Adults, Photography, anything else you'd like to pay me to do...If you want to speak to me I can consult w/ you for a whole hour@20.00 an hour...Thank You very much...

Have A Beautiful Day wherever you **ARE**! I work by the hour @ 10.68 an hour per project. **30% DOWN PLEASE! THANK YOU VERY MUCH**...I know, I know, you read this far. **CONGRATULATIONS! YOU'RE A WINNER! CONGRATULATIONS, YOU'RE A WINNER!!! SO AM I...I BELIEVE IN YOU, I LOVE YOU FOR WHOM YOU ARE**...Keep On Truckin' - Eddie Kendricks...

COME DOWN to DEERING OAKS Sat Jun 16, 2017 7am-6pm to **C-E-L-E-B-R-A-T-E PRIDE 2017**! I'll be selling my funky cool shirts to raise money for a trip out west. Will also be selling stickers & bead necklaces [**1st 100 people**: **FREE BONUS** sticker or bead necklace]. My table will be located near the bandstand area. I'll be wearing my clown wig & sunglasses. Come On Down to make that purchase today! **3 BONUSES** for buying funky fun t-shirt you can wear anywhere you like. **H.E.L.P.** ...

Cancel Your Subscriptions to anybody who brings you drama. You don't need that!

Jokes You Can Use On People:

I'M THE WORST COMEDIAN IN THE WORLD, that's why people laugh at my jokes:

We live in a Society where people use an $800 smart phone to check their food stamp balance

Ashley Lenartson that is so correct...who wants an 800 phone. I've bought so many phones that I must have spent 800 on phones by now...most of them are going to a battered woman's or men's shelter but you can't stop somebody from abusing you so why have a cell phone for protection??? So you can hit them over the head with it to distract them when they are physically abusing **YOU** then run like the dickens...

Here's a joke meant to go no further: I could put Olive Oil on my face or hemorrhoid cream on it to tighten it up...or I could put hemorrhoid cream on my hole to make it tighter...you just never know. There are a lot of uses for hemorrhoid cream...hope you are laughing you butt off...I surely am a Comedian...I mean Cumedian...now if I could just stop touching myself I'd be alright...

Some people like looking like **PRUNES**: they look like they are trying to dehydrate rather than hydrate themselves. It's called Drug Addiction or just growing older ungracefully…

Today is **NO CLOTHES DAY**

Today is **NO UNDERWEAR DAY**

Beau Tox is a friend of mine. He's related to **De Tox**...

Do you save bacon fat? If so, why and when would you use it? I'd use the bacon fat to grease up my girlfriend then go to town on her.

We are all animals. Some of us more so than others. Or, how about Monsters??? Check under your bed for the Monsters...

I'll put a SMILE on YOUR FACE...drop trousers...

There is no guarantee that love comes easy, but there is a guarantee that love comes sleazy…

I Need Pussy - what is pussy??? A woman's pussy or an asspussy??? **Which is tighter**: the pussy or the ass??? It's just a question to ponder for the day...said by John Burns on facebook: that all depends on which has been fuct more: the pussy or the ass…it's blown out mangled jangled beef curtains that looks like a trainwreck…

Ricky Davis says - Okay you know how you eat chicken with your fingers so is it wrong to eat porterhouse steak with your fingers keep in mind you're at home with the to-go porterhouse steak.
Answer: do what you want however, I must warn you that when you eat chicken make sure that it doesn't wiggle around in the plate after it is played with and when you eat a to-go Porterhouse Steak make sure that it is cooked well done and that you put your Special Sauces in the Porterhouse Steak before you eat it, if you know what I mean.

I'm a talented Artist w/ a B.A. in Art from The University of Small Minds, I mean Smart Minds and I also attended The Portland School of Mostly White Artists back in the day...

Some guy on facebook asked me where I am from: this was my standard reply for a gorgeous Saturday outside...two days in a row...I said, "My mammy and pappy." He was not amused!

What is frosting for 500 Alex???

Jesus wept because he was a very sad individual: He had bi-polar disorder. That's why he wept

I want your cum in my asshole desperately: when do you want to get married guy???

You can cum visit me and suck my cock dry every nite: let me know when we're tying the KNOT!!!

Pickles 'N Po Boys: which is better? The pickles or the po boys???

Fuck You Silly: when

Where's my captain on a Snowy White Horse? Steve? He fell off the horse and broke a heel...

A new product on the market: cover up pants: who would have thunk it

Talking Heads??? I know your feelings are all located in your asshole...that's why it twitches when you are sleeping at night and then it opens up and says, "**FEED ME MORE COCK, FEED ME MORE COCK**" Have a lovely lay...I see no offers on the table so I'm considering this conversation **DONE**! Bye Felatio!!!

Here's your cock pix of the day: **ENJOY**: will it fill your gaping hole or do something you never thought it would do: You need a bigger one to do that like a **Horse Penis**???

I can't wait until I'm dead: I'm so sick of seeing these gd posts about needing help: **WTF!** facebook has every walk of life on here doesn't it??? Can you tell I'm in a **Polly Pissy Mood**???

Sometimes I feel like I come from another planet...it gets so tired with people making requests for this that and the other thing and it ain't over 'til the fat lady or fat man sings his or her tunes...

David Laskey thru facebook:
Time to get ready for a **Block Party** to see what it's about: its safe so don't think the wrong thing ok everybody have a good day:
Ashley Lenartson's reply:
It's so much fun blocking people who think I want to write back to them all the time and send them dirty pix...one can only do that so often and then **BAM!!!** they end up being **BLOCKED PERMANENTLY**...**I'd rather go to a BLOCK PARTY TO GET DRUNK AT THIS POINT IN TIME TODAY**...

Looking for a female texting partner (Portland, Maine thru Craigslist)

Currently stranded ran out of gas. Can someone please help? (Portland, Maine)

Looking for upright jazz bassist looking for uptight jazz bassist is what I read

Beaver Cove: I wonder what kinds of beavers can be found in Beaver Cove, Maine??? Anybody, you ma'am you look like a beaver lover. How about you sir???

I told a Psychic "thanks for making me laugh" They replied, "I hear that you do that a lot when you look in the mirror."

August 9th is in 9 hours: I think I'm going to cum just from hearing that

Snow White has morphed into a man: must be those Dwarfs at it **AGAIN...**

I've been hiding from exercise. I'm in the **Fitness Protection Program**

Just made the cover of '**Rogue Weekly**' as I'm a roving fat pig and I love myself at any weight I gain or lose…

Patrons of The Arts = Patrons of The Farts

Who wants to see me put all of my clothes back on? Anybody? Oh, everybody so they can laugh their asses off about me being **NAKED ON STAGE**…I get it, I get it…

Does he spread easy??? Maybe when you smear whipt cream all over him

Does she spread easy??? Maybe when you put Nutella on her

Self-Esteem = Self-Esteemy

I'm pregnant *AGAIN*…must be all those jelly donuts that I've been eating for breakfast

Bye Bye Baby Love = Bi Bi Baby Love

Caucasion = Cockasians

Caucasions = Cock Asians...what do Asian have to do with this hole story??? I don't get it...why haven't they been dragged through the proverbial mud??? Am I missing something... https://tinyurl.com/d4msmg8 The Filthy Funny Dirty Joke Book - Professor PMS **Go Now Laugh Your A** Off** and be prepared to be insulted and laugh at or with me anyways...I know the "**White Man**" is being blamed for destroying the rest of the world and people who live in this Country but come on, it's not all true what they say about White People: you have to look beyond the color of a persons' skin in order to work with them and overlook most of the Jealousy going on here...LAUGH YOUR A** OFF TODAY @ LEAST 50++ TIMES...that's what I do to maintain any sense of "NORMLCY". You do the same...

Smooches and Starbucks! Ariana Grande and Pete Davidson Share a Kiss During Day Out in N.Y.C.

FIGHTING...that's when a new plan has to be **HATCHED**...who knew he has a **BIG SAUSAGE**. I wish I had a bigger sausage as then I woodn't need to leave my home and I'd be practicing **ONANISM = SELF LOVE**...I know, I know...and she claims that she's **NEVER BEEN FUCT**??? **MAYBE** like the Geico commercial says **MAYBE**: Do you know how to suck a penis: **MAYBE**...I'm sure she's going to give him 'All That She Wants is another baby'...I sure hope so...if it's true that she's been saving all of her love for the right guy then he's going to breaking into her **Three Lock Box**...

The only reason I came out of the closet was because the doors fell off

Why are there so many scammers in my feed (facebook): **Barrett Dylan Davis** I can tell you why if you PayPal me $20 **Ashley Lenartson** My reply: HA HA HA HA HA HA HA…

James Pike Ashley Lenartson
It seems that you can't take a joke.

This is proof:
I try to be serious and others think I'm joking and when I'm joking, people think I'm serious.

That is just sad...

Why are real people so hard to find??? Why can't everyone chill and love everyone???
Because most human beings are **DAMAGED GOODS LOCATED IN THE DISCOUNT SECTION OF THE SUPERMARKET**

With all the **SCAMMERS** on facebook it is getting very difficult to keep up with all the **REAL MEN**. Please say **HELLO**: I didn't know there were any real men on this site…

I was conceived through Anal Sex: I turned out alright!!!!!!!

Your hole is too much: It's an **ENDLESS BUFFET**

Juggling = juggling balls

SHUT UP = when somebody tells me to shut the fuck up I just start laughing HARDER!!!

Where are you from? My mother and father

Do you have any family you are close to: never, I'm an orphan: my names Little Orphan Beau Peep and I'm wild in the streets and between the sheets of Portland, Maine

If only I Could Turn Back Time – You might get a glimpse of CHER

Little House on The Prairie = Little House on The Fairy

Personal Ads: Single Female Archaeologist prefers carbon dating. Prefers older men.

Surprises = Slurprises

is that smiley face mentally challenged and very happy about it???

My name's **NOBODY** and I'm located in the middle of the ocean: I'm a man without a country...

What is your name? Polly Anna thru facebook

The Most Sobering Political Scandal in American History – I didn't know I was drunk from all this small talk in the Satanized Media

Saucy! = Pizza

Does he come with the furniture or come on it??? Either way...

BIG BASKET

Ven(t)i vidi vici = I saw, I vented, I conquered, I came

Oh Lord, so glad I'm out = Oh Lord, so glad I got **OUTED**

Fantabulous is what the organist said after he finished the program for the day

THE Church Organist: I'd like to play your Organ. Will you teach me?

Can sing in your choir

I'm sure that when I put my organ in you you will sing much better...

What are you doing tonight? Licking your asshole

What do you do for a living: I fuck people in the ass. How old are you: old enough to know better

I'm not Trans, I'm Pans...I'm not gay, straight, bi-bi love, lesbian, transsexual or transvestite, I just go for what I like.
He wants to get married but he don't wanna marry me: that's because he's not ready to cummit as he already did that!

But but but = butt butt butt everywhere and in my face

Comedian = A Cumedian with emphasis on the cum: cum again…I insist you do it

let me know what you saw and what you bought today...Have a beautiful day...Go Now...so pretty: it's like looking at a delicate flower in the fields...I want to pick you up and hold you in my arms and never let you go...

Yes I am missing a cock in my mouth do you want to see the nude pics of me I'll send them to you if you'll send me some of you

Go right ahead: you will be better able to give fabulass bjs after those teeth are taken out of you and more

Somebody who does flooring for a living told me to stop sending photos of myself and what I'm selling on and offline:
I told them, "I haven't been sending you any naked pix so don't worry about a thing."

Let me know what you saw and possibly spent your whole paycheck on...

I'm good: Are you a good girl or a rotten girl when you don't get your way???

I want to eat your mangina out and then some…sign me right up…I can't get enough ass pussy in my face that is clean and tight…

I'm Mary from the Facebook board based in USA

"the last annual concluded draw that was held by Facebook to help people your profile was selected among the fifteen lucky winners who won the sum of nine hundred thousand dollars" "oh goody, goody, goody: where do I send the check and when do I pick up the rest of my winnings...let me know how much of a fee I have to pay to claim my winnings." **Delete delete delete delete delete & block permanently.** Anybody who works with facebook and claims to be with facebook on my facebook page is obviously a Con-Artist.

Psychotherpist = Psycho Thera Pissed...it costs a lot of money to be stuck in anal-y-sis...120 an hour and you only get 12 sessions when you are working your way thru the system…

why thanks very much: it helps to be loved, not hated...but then again, I'm used to that by now...a small dick is better than no dick at all...can you imagine what it would be like not to have a penis at all but a pussy between your legs: I'd love it...with my luck I'd probably end up attracting an abusive man with a horsedick who likes slapping me around any chance he gets and telling me to spread my gash so he can fuck the shit out of me in both of my holes: grateful I'm a good little boy who swallows every drop presented to him...butt, I have no time for abuse unless I get paid to be abused…tain't dat duh truth…

Life is like bondage: Bondage (being tied up or tied down with ropes or imaginary ropes), Discipline (has to do with the Disciples of Jesus, etc. and doing what you are told to do, not what you think you should do - not religious by any stretch of the imagination - used to be a **Spiritualist**, not so anymore), Sadism (being mean to self and others for the right reasons) and Masochism (allowing the "abuse" to take place) with the consent [cuntscent] of two willing Adults...

Is that a flying saucer behind your head...very nice pix with the low light...?

Welcome = Wel cum

My real name is Little Beau Peep and I'm wild in the streets of Portland, Maine

Dama Ardiente
"There's nothing that you can't overcome with God on your side." Ashley Lenartson said, "What happens when God isn't on your side and the Devil is trying to burn your house down???"

Are you a Devil?
Chat Conversation End

Hello

I fall in love with you can I get
your pictures
Hello are u there

That is why I like falling in love
with the Devil

Are you a Devil
Chat Conversation End

Talking Dirty to People

   I'll help break you in like a Disney Ride: gentle at 1st then take you to **POUNDTOWN, USA: I'm the be(a)st, you be THE BEST**...I like eating out a hot man pussy and then getting it ready for my big bocho. You know the rest is your story to tell people about when you want to talk about getting finger banged by a guy who knows what he is doing: the secret to getting plowed in the fields of Maine: breathing, liking the pain and then the pleasure of getting fucked harder and liking to have a great time with somebody who likes hot manpussy...that's right:

You've got a hot manpussy between those hot lithe legs of yours...let me know when you'd like to get together for some hot action...**207-450-3140** I'm like a **Disney Ride**: once you get on you want to get off and then you want to get right back on for another ride...my names "**Bucking Bronco**" from Portland, Maine: Howdy Doody???!!! I'm well, you be well, let's have some hot fun in the **Summertime**...or at any time of the year...

Year = Qear

The dirtier, the better: hot sex in the **Summertime**...oh yeah baby, just ride me like a bucking bronco...

Ghost Pepper Cock...who wants to try **<u>THAT</u>**??? I DO, I DO...

I'll believe that when you show up at my door with your **Moby Dick** in your hands saying **FEED ME MORE, FEED ME MORE**: I'm going to rip off my clothes and Ben Dover and tell you to get the 'F in here...

Do you remember your 1st job? My 1st job was sucking daddy off in the back of the rambler car he owned and he'd give me a pack of gum for doing it...it was fun fun **<u>FUN</u>** 'til he had a heart attack while I was sucking him off and then I had to start taking care of him to nurse him back to good health...

Note to self:

Just because it pops into my head does NOT mean it should come out of my mouth.

It's so easy to confuse everybody with one's behavior: Straight Guys won't admit to being '**Gay**' but they will admit to being '**Straight**' and still suck a guy's c*ck and some even take it up their mangina...that's life: they go where the hot mouth or a** is...I'm just sayin'…you can call yourself any label you like or none at all as '<u>**Labels belong on Jars**</u>'.

Sgt. Pepper's Lonely Hearts Club Band = Sgt. Pecker's Lonely Hearts Club Band

Lonely Hearts = Lonely Fearts vs Alone In The Universe: which do you prefer: I prefer being alone with my thoughts: I feel better when I'm all alone and I'm ok with that. I really am. So what, I live alone: things could be much worse than they really are…they really could be…

I was trying to be transparent to my parents and tried killing myself but that didn't work. So here I am. They weren't thankful that I survived my 1st Suicide attempt. WTF! Is wrong with parents these days??? I'll tell you what: letting their children spend too much time with their laptops, cell phones and other devices instead of having a decent conversation about what it means to be alive…

What do you call two queers named Bob? Oral Roberts

IRREVERENT, IMPERFECT & INSATIABLE …PREFECTLY FLAWED…

BEST IN THE WORLD COMEDY

We live in a Society where people use an $800 smart phone to check their food stamp balance Ashley Lenartson that is so correct...who wants an $800 phone. I've bought so many phones that I must have spent $800 on phones by now...most of them are going to a battered men's shelter but you can't stop somebody from abusing you so why have a cell phone for protection??? It's much better to buy a tazer so that you can get away from your abuser or a baseball bat to take him out when he does attack you.

Rasputin had a 13" penis: what am I going to do with a 13" penis??? Just what am I going to do??? Have a lot of fun fun FUN all the time and charge by the inch. How much of my 13" penis can you afford today???

That's a joke meant to further: I could put Olive Oil on my face or hemorrhoid cream on it to tighten up my whole face...or I could put hemorrhoid cream on my hole to make it tighter...you just never know. There are a lot of uses for hemorrhoid cream these days...hope you are laughing you butt off...I surely am a Comedian...I mean Cumedian...now if I could just stop touching myself I woodn't be so obsessed with spanking my Monkey. He gets so angry at me that he spits at me and then tries to attack me...I gave Hemorrhoid Cream & Ex-Lax to my relatives and former friends for Christmas. They didn't get the joke. What's up with that???

Take Ex-Lax when you need to Re-Lax

Some people like looking like **PRUNES**

Supplicant = Supplecunt

Dictator = Dick Tater, pleased ta' meat 'ya

Addicted = Addickted

Today is **NO CLOTHES DAY**

Today is **NO UNDERWEAR DAY = be prepared for the chaffing that comes from not wearing your underwear all the time. Better get some cold cream to put between your legs**

Beau Tox is a friend of mine: he's related to Big Cox...they get along quite well with each other: They're brothers

Do you save bacon fat? If so, why and when would you use it? I'd use the bacon fat to grease up my girlfriend then go to town on her. Then I can ask her to make grunting noises just like a pig when I bang her. Oh, that's right; she's going to be making grunting noises on account of my really big horse penis...

We are all animals. Some of us more than others. Or, how about Monsters??? My good friend, Lisa D. says, "I'm not a monster." She's technically correct as she looks like THE Pillsbury Dough Girl, The Michelin Woman or Humpty Dumpty. Hey, I'm just sayin': I don't mind having sex with a fat person…the fatter the better: more pushin' for the cushion

I want to become pregnant for different reasons but definitely not from raw octopus...Cephalopods got trapped in a woman's mouth and attached themselves to the inside of her mouth (gums, tongue & cheek) **spermatophores** (a cup of semen from the ejaculatory apparatus which ejaculate sperm into her mouth) attached themselves because of a cement like substance and grew into baby octopuses and came crawling out of her mouth as people in the East eat raw octopus (**lesson**: do not eat raw octopus unless it's your girlfriend's pussy or your boyfriend's mangina). Yup, she got pregnant in her mouth. In the West the raw organs are removed so this can't happen. She became an Octomom. Or, is it **Octopussy** with baby octopi in her mouth...NASTY! NASTY! NASTY! Remind me not to eat **RAW OCTOPUS IN ANOTHER COUNTRY** or even this country...

Country = Cuntry

I've known 3 males in my life who got molested: they loved it. Why hate something that happened to you? It's not going to help you to stay angry about what happened to you so long ago: did you enjoy it or are you just going to find an excuse to be angry for the rest of your life??? You will only spend your life being cut off from '**Source Energy**'. Just accept what happened to you and move on. After all, it takes 2 people to get molested, not just the molester. It also takes **YOU**. You could have said, "NO!" at some point in the game...I'm just sayin'...I never got molested growing up but I do know people who did and they're so pissed off at the person who molested them. I don't have time for anger/rage issues.

A white woman called police on black people barbecuing. This is how the community responded: they had a giant BBQ and invited friends from near and far to participate in the fun and festivities…

I pissed in my mama's face when I was a baby.

I shit all over my step-father when I was a baby.

I like fun and romance = I like cum & blomance

I just went on a fishing trip with my boyfriend. I unzipped his pants and started sucking on his pole. I was the bait.

He said, She said = what did anybody say? There are always two sides to every story. Whenever two people fighting with each other ask me to take sides I just defer and say, "I know you are correct." And then, when the other side comes to me, "I know you are correct." Then I just walk away. It's not up to me to be the referee. I don't want to get caught up in a dirty little war between two people who cannot make amends with each other. F that!!!

Kaitlyn Jenner has a 21 year old girlfriend. What's up with THAT???!!! Nothing like having a younger person as your gf or bf…that's what money and power does for a 70 year old transsexual…

<u>'Show Dogs' removes 2 'troubling' scenes amid criticism</u>

I'm a Show Dog. How come nobody has touched **MY PRIVATE PARTS**??? What happened **THERE**??? **NOTHING**! I want somebody to touch my private parts. After all, most men are dogs in heat...I won't kiss or tell...so are most women. They just won't admit it when you ask them such a personal question.

Same goes for a lot of other animals: If a female rat doesn't reproduce then she is more likely to develop tumors and those need to be taken care of at the Vet Office. If the rat has a cold and he or she has those little red dots come out of their nose when they cough get it taken care of as it is something that they catch at an early age when they are babies...so, I can see what J.P. is saying...ok now, who's ready to manually release a male dog to maintain its "testicular and prostate health"??? Anybody...People use any excuse these days to get their panties in a twist instead of educating people about the real dangers of not masturbating their pets manually: if it needs to be done for a reason or another...**<u>Sexual Abuse</u>** is rampant in Society. Only a few people actually get caught. Everybody else just gets to keep on doing what they are doing until they are caught in the act. Such a shame...it really IS...or is it???

Most people have bi-polar disorder: you just don't find out about it until you get screamed at by them: by then it's much too late.

<u>Caitlyn Jenner fires shade at Kardashians and Trump in wide-ranging interview</u>

I'd rather be on the cover of a **<u>Fruit Loops</u>** Box than **<u>Wheaties</u>** any day of the week as I am a little bit fruity in the loops but just as addictive as the nasty cereal with all the fake ingredients that make me sick and addicted to sugar and milk. No wonder kids are crazy: all that sugar in the morning makes a kid listless at school and not able to study properly...especially the day after Halloween

The Pampered Chef Party = The Pampered Chef: I'm so glad a chef is wearing Pampers to his party…

What is a Twatwaffle = the **idiot** that gets on your last **damn** nerve. The person you know that suffers from excessive verbal diarrhea. The one you want to **smack** in the face with a pick-axe. The person who has done it all and done it better than you. There is this twatwaffle in my anatomy class who won't shut up **even though** he is obviously an **idiot** and everyone fucking hates his sputtering face.

I think hiring about a maid way too often for someone who has plenty of time to clean. **Solution**: Hire a maid to clean in the **NUDE**. That way you will have somebody to ogle at while they are cleaning your house in the nude. And, it better be somebody who is gorgeous looking or it's not going to work out at all…

"People should mind their own business." I think that's the funniest thing that I have read on facebook. Since when do people know how to mind their **OWN** business???

DIET DAY 1: I've removed all the bad food from the house. It was delicious…now; I'm going to binge and purge to get it out of my system

Which one of you guys put **pornhub** up on the refrigerator at Home Depot???

HAND JOB, better than nothin'…

The Glitter Coffin Company: now there's a company that makes coffins that people will want to buy at a solemn time of ones passing

"I'll get you pussyface, and your little dog, too!!!"

Well, scratch my happy ass, its Friday…said the donkey…

There are doorways to demonic possession: Heavy Metal, Burning Man Festival, Religion, and Eating Food with chemicals in it, etc. etc.

Somebody's going to eat my man pussy tonight? Excellent! Can't wait to taste dinner...

My friend caught one of John Waters' pencil mustaches at one of his shows. That's great. I have a pencil dick. I use it to write with it. It's a gel glitter dick. I like to write all over people's faces with it.

Don't bother trying this if you are a Democrat or a man who is gay. I'm not a Democrat and I'm Gay as in HAPPY...thanks for asking...

A bitch is a bitch is a bitch is a bitch...enjoy being bitchy...

Arnold Schwarzenegger's favorite words: "I'm coming, I'm coming". He used to say that anytime he got on a talk show in the 70's like **The Mike Douglas Show** or The **Merv Griffin Show**

I just got back from Hell. It's wonderful this time of the year. Things are just starting to heat up…**<u>AGAIN</u>**: Summer's coming…

<u>**Exploitation**</u>: What does that really mean…"we exploited the people of the African Plains and they prospered thanks to us? So what we took advantage of them. They're better off than they were so we must have done something good even if that means we took advantage of them and changed their way of life." And, ripped them off and told them what to plant and grow. After all, it's the "**Western Way of Life**"…ganging up on people all over the planet and making them do what we want them to do. It's do as I tell you to do or **DIE MOTHERFUCKER**!!!

Feed me more: what do you want me to feed you? My dick, ass or balls???

What girl wants to fuck you when you told her she's not fuckable? Peggy W.

THE Thought Police: just who are the 'thought police' and what do they really want???

Police Brutality: just what IS Police Brutality??? Most people who join the Police Farce are "**Wannabee Cops**" w/ bullying issues. That's why they are there: they like controlling **YOU**!!!

A fridgerator versus a fag: at least when you pull your meat out of the fridge it doesn't fart but when you pull your meat out of someone's ass it farts. What's up with **<u>THAT</u>**???!!!

Indian Jokes: What kind of a room does an Indian make at a hotel? A reservation. What is an Indian's favorite pop song: Indian Reservation. Why do Indians stay on Reservations? How the heck would I know, I'm not an Indian.

Double stuffed pizza: sometimes I feel like a Double Stuffed Pizza

I'm a racist chocolate eater

Have you lost your looks: what kind of person asks anybody that question??? Have you lost your Virginity yet??? This is the question I asked Sandra H. and she had no answer for that question. I wonder why??? I know her from another life: she's very testy when she wants to get that way. We don't get along in this life.

This = Dis

Prejudice, Hatred & Bigotry by Maverick Ashlee Lenartson

Tough Love: just what is **TOUGH LOVE**??? I'd rather have tough nuts so I can get the job done.

The All Seeing Eye: The Eye In The Sky

Truth and Light: so hard to come by these days as a lot of people get their panties in a twist for the slightest reason that has nothing to do with the subject at hand.

Just Kidding: no you were not

Dumpster Diving: who doesn't like going Dumpster Diving? You never know what you are going to find that somebody threw out that's still good to eat, a brand new microwave oven or even a dining room set.

I don't smoke but I like to start fires: that's why I tell people things that aren't true. The most fun anybody will ever have is telling somebody a lie and watching how long it takes to get back to the person who told it so they can have a great chuckle: of course the person who finds that out is going to go off on **YOU**. Isn't it a pitty??? Did you know I'm related to **Chuckles The Clown**???

I Didn't Know or I Don't Know **_IS_** a blessing

Cheap, cheap, cheap, cheap, cheap = what the bird said when it didn't want to pay its bill

Mind = A Mind Is A Terrible Thing To Taste. It's even more terrible to waste. Most people stop learning in High School around the age of 16-18. That's because they are bored out of their skulls and want to do something fun & exciting like f*ck, get high or go to a party at '**The Top of The World**'. That's a place that exists in Eagle Lake, Maine. I've never been there. I should have gone up when I was a teenager. I really should have.

Big Brothers: what exactly are Big Brothers???

Big Mothers: what exactly are Big Mothers???

I took my annual bath: I told that to a friend and she was flabbergasted when I said it. I didn't quite know what I was saying as I thought an annual bath happened once per week but it doesn't, it happens once a lifetime. Or, who would like to give me my Annual Bath as it's like giving an Annual Report in front of a group of people.

It's not who you know, it's who you blow to get the job. Yeah Right! No **Casting Couch** here…that's not necessary…

A Big Fish Story: what exactly is a big fish story?

A Big Yarn: I told a really big yarn at The Annual Knitting Festival

My Maiden Name: Miss or Mister

Tommy Gun: just exactly what is a Tommy Gun???

Tripolar Disorder is what I have. It's definitely not bi-polar disorder. It's Tri-Polar: I'll try anything once and if I like it twice.

The Pissed of Great White Hope: Bob Hope, a shark, a???

What would Jesus do? He'd become a martyr as that's his fate: Jesus was an Alien from what I've read online but one mustn't believe everything they read online these days.

Unlovely, Unlovely, Unforgivable: SIN

Peace amidst the storm: Shitstorm 2018

The Secret war on cash: there's definitely a secret war on cash: just make sure you don't have too much on you when you travel in West Virginia on Amtrak train services.

Why do you have to be careful when it's raining cats and dogs? So you don't step in them

Why was the court all wet? Because they kept dribbling on it

Take care of yourself: witch self. I feel like Sybil today

Proud Bater: just what is a **Proud Bater**??? A "**Master Debater**"??? An alligator???

The Poor Artists Campaign: make a donation today: Maverick Ashlee Lenartson 198 Sherwood St 3 Portland, ME 04103 **Just Do It**: I'll make sure to thank you much later.

Every day is a holiday

Memorial Day: Memwhorial Day, a day that you get laid by your girlfriend

When is Father's Day: every day of the year

Easy: my middle name or a Commodores song

Winner: Maverick Ashlee Lenartson a/k/a Oh Little Beau Peep or Little Beau Peepsters

Congratulations, You're A Winner: now make me laugh harder so I can piss my pants!!!

Bonus = Boneass: who wants their boneass today??? Wood you like to see a boneass today? How about a bone in an ass??? My bone??? My bone is like a piece of hard wood in the morning or before I get to bed at night…

For Real = 'Fo Real

You Tube vs Blow Tube

Dick Butkuss = Dick Buttkiss

Life Is Short, Enjoy It: make sure that you laugh your ass off 50 times per day.

I Like Other People's Money

Twitter is for Twits who Tweet on Twitter all day long…

If it wasn't for my funny sense of humor…I wouldn't be funny at all…I have a funny bone: I laugh when I hit my funny bone…

Controversial: I'm controversial as I make people actually **<u>THINK</u>** after they laugh at my jokes I tell up on stage!

Will you wipe my ass??? I was just in a car accident and my name is Mo **<u>THE</u>** Ho…

I'm Perfect As I Am

TPT = Trailer Park Trash

TPR = Toilet Paper

Jokes For Assholes

Parents got fucking molested by their older children who became Adults: what a shocker

Fucked Cams Are Us

DO DO DO DO DO: I Do, I Do, I Do, I Do, I Do

Projectile Vomiting: it happens to the best of us

Kick him in the ding ding

My Private Life Is None of Your Business

I'm an **Idiot Savant**

Lobotomy: more people should have lobotomies to make the world a safer place to live in

Wannabe: Donald W.F., Tim N., Maverick Ashlee Lenartson

"**Chill Out**" said the refrigerator to the meat that was just put in it

Have Fun…AGAIN!
Bugs: what did one bug say to another bug? Don't bug me

When I was growing up my mother would say, "You are the product of two cabooses bumping together in 1962."

Botched: I am the product of a botched childhood and a botches nose surgery in Massatwoshits

I AM = I Yam

The Pink Panther: Maverick Ashlee Lenartson

I'm going to start a **'Go Fuck Me Page':** who's with me???

My Dead Aunt = My Dead Ant

Nuclear = Nu Clear: why do we need more Nuclear Plants: to make the world more toxic??? It don't make any sense…

Fake News: Donald J. Trump is the product of **<u>FAKE NEWS</u>**.

Self-driving cars: what could possibly go wrong with self-driving cars? **A person jay walking their bike across the road and getting killed.**

Arcel Aleno asked me how old I was: I said, "55 years going on 2 years of age: stuck in the anal retentive stage...I never stopped growing..."

God is good god is great God loves it when I masturbate

The Two Faces of Eve: Bette Davis, Joan Crawford (Crawfish)

The Whip: let it whip baby

Why I'm here: because my mother and father couldn't stop fucking each other in 1962

Delivery = Dewivewy

B Good Comedy!!!

Potato = potatoh

Tomato = tomatoh

I'll take Big Balls for 500, Alex

'Yo Mama said di'nt

I Got Soul: I have Potty Mouth Disease

Too Open: Maverick Ashlee Lenartson

You never know when you gonna have to turn into a ho'

What's up Chuck??? Did you up chuck again

I sell so much more when I put out

STUD = I put the STUD back in s.t.d.

A sense of humor is required to get through life

I act like a 2 year old most of the time

Fifty = fitty sity or sety

Why do mermaids wear seashells? They are too big for "B" shells, and too small for "D" shells.

What did the turtle do when he ran out of gas? He went to the Shell station.

What's a turtle's favorite thrill ride? Shell Shock

Take It All: take what of all???

Temptation Island: who wouldn't want to move to 'Temptation Island'? I'd rather be centered deep in my soul…thank you very much: **Temptation Island** is a very dangerous place for somebody who doesn't have the balls not to be tempted…

Grog: Alcoholic beverages. Who has an alcoholic beverage for me after the show???

A ho is a ho is a HO

De Nile River Egypt, Maine or **De Nial River, Egypt, Maine**

Bankruptcy: when the bank goes under because of mismanagement

Collection Agency: an agency that collects money from people deceptively: never give your money to a collection agency as your debt has already been **SOLD** and bought by another company trying to make money off of your debt. If you are going to pay off your older debt then pay the actual company if they are still in business…

Whales are older than the hills

Older than the hills: my girlfriend is older than the hills

Daddy: exactly what is a DADDY?

Mama: my mama said

Dada: an art piece from a certain Century

Mama: an art piece from another Century

Honey Bunches of Oh's: oh really

Big Brother: I do want to see him in my boudoir

Big Mother: A highly pissed off relative who is jealous of the new mother

A **BIG** Fish Story [make gesture]

Why did the skeleton not go to the dance? He had no body to go with

White Power: when you have cocaine smeared all over your face

Skirt: do blow hot air up my skirt

Underwear: under who???

Morgan Freeman is a free man

Blind Masturbation: masturbation that makes you go blind

Why did the bread commit suicide? It was living the crumby life or it got old and full of mold

Jungle Bunny: there are an awful lot of Jungle Bunnys running around here and not all of them are black

Idiots: Welcome to Idiotland, Maine or Welcome to Idiotland as there are an awful lot of idiots running around out there

Reincarnation Drink Mix: Jim Jones Kool Aid???

I need t p for my p p and bungholio

A web site: http://shirtsyoushouldntbebuyingtoday.blogspot.com 92% of my friends buy my work and wear it on their back. Most people would agree that I'm a talented Artist. Go Now, Check Us Out Today. Goal: Selling 99 Shirts Today. You'll be glad that you bought our merchandise to make you Happier.

Goodbye, it's been nice knowing you = Goodbye, it's been nice blowing you

Hairy armpits are making a comeback. Do you love it or hate it? On facebook Ashley Lenartson Why should I care??? It's always about women...I'm sick of it...they can flaunt whatever they want but don't say anything nice to them or you might find yourself on the wrong end of a lawsuit for sexual harassment...

You can't force somebody to be Patriotic about reciting the Pledge of Allegiance. We live in a Republic. That's why the NFL looks stupid forcing employees to do so! Take a knee? Take a fist? Its ok, the players can afford to take a knee when they do not want to stand up for 'The Pledge of Allegiance'

NO NO NO the **HO** won't go!

Life is too expensive for one to play or just joke with life: Life is too expensive not to have a sense of humor...

You ate that for fuckfest this morning, huh??? I bet it was sweet tasting bunghole...sweet meat...

What are you on tonight: raging whoremoans???

Isn't that what a backseat driver is all about: I've got something to put in their mouths that will keep them occupied...?

Cowcunta, Maine: it's everywhere: the more white sugar, white bread and white dairy (yes, it's full of puss) you ingest the fatter you will get at any age.

Hot Cocksucker: just exactly what is a hot cocksukka??? Somebody who likes going down on other men…ex. The Cocksucker Express is leaving any minute now

Baby On Board: who's baby???

Naval Aviator = Evil Aviator

DISQUALIFIED: for breaking the rules

Take A Knee = Take A Cock: which wood you rather do??? I'd rather take a cock any day of the week up me arse. The only position I'm allowed to play on any football team is **Tite End**. BTW, it's a <u>**FREE COUNTRY**</u>

Daddy's Day: that's the day you kiss his ass for knocking your mother up!

Mother…**load**

Versions = Virgins

Idiot University: how many people have been to Idiot University: ANYBODY???!!!

6 Man Tag Team Action…sounds pornographic to me no matter how I lick at it: or, is it **6 Man Fag Team Action**: either way it's going to get hot in here

I Can't Even Think Straight: that's because I'm G-A-Y

Samoa Joe = Samoa Blo or Samoa Ho

Facial…I need a '**Cum Facial**' to revive myself: **r e j u v I n a t e**

Keep On Sucking…until you get it right

I have a new brother…his name is **Tinker Bell**: he's related to Michael Jackson. You know Michael was the <u>**ORIGINAL**</u> **'TINKER BELL' of the 20th Century**

Master Debaters Degree or Master Baters Degree: I have both degrees as I'm the best at what I do even when I fail miserably!!! It's ok to fail until I get it right the 50th time or the 100th time.

Morgan Freeman: does the Sexual Harassment of women by men ever stop? Why do women have to wait 20-30 years to file a suit against somebody famous? You'd think they would have filed suit when it happened. So much for the 'Statute of Limitations'. I guess it never runs out when it comes to women being sexually harassed by men because if a woman wants to get even she'll do it. So what she just ruined your career in Hollywood, get it Holly Wood…take a seat on the 'Casting Couch'

It hurt like hell but it felt good at the same time: I like pain…give me all you've got and I'll dodge your raging bullets…

www.ingramcontent.com/pod-product-compliance
Lightning Source LLC
Chambersburg PA
CBHW041232050726
47599CB00007B/927